JUKAN-DO KARATE

Joseph A. Leonard

authorHOUSE®

AuthorHouse™
1663 Liberty Drive, Suite 200
Bloomington, IN 47403
www.authorhouse.com
Phone: 1-800-839-8640

First published by AuthorHouse 6/15/2009

ISBN: 978-1-4389-5392-2 (sc)

Printed in the United States of America
Bloomington, Indiana

This book is printed on acid-free paper.

FOR WORLD DISTRIBUTION
Published by Jiyukido Martial Arts Fed.
P.O. Box 7626
S.T. Thomas V.I. 00801

CONTENTS

Part I Introduction

Part 2 Calisthenics

Part 3 Hand & Fist Pushups

Part 4 Hand & Finger Exercise

Part 5 Windmill Exercise

Part 6 Leg Lifts

Part 7 Hop, Jump, and Crawl

Part 8 Flat Back Situps

Part 9 Floor Leg Stretch

THE WAY OF TEN

1. DISCIPLINE
2. BASIC
3. SELF-DEFENSE
4. KATA
5. SPARRING
6. BO STAFF
7. ESCRIMA STICKS
8. SAMURAI SWORD
9. SLIDING BLOCK-PUNCHING
10. THROW1NG TECHNIQUES

What the mind lears it will always remember, but what the body practice it might forget. You must train your body to equal that of your mind.

Master Joseph A. Leonard

50 Years of Martial Arts Involvement.
President and Founder of the Jiyukido Martial Arts Federation.
Founder and Developer of the JuKan-Do Karate System.
Inducted into the World Martial Arts Hall of Fame in 2002.
Registered in U.S.A. Shotokan Karate.

FOREWORD

I practice Free Style Karate in Bridgeport Conn. in 1958 with members of the Y.M.C.A. and the Bridgeport Boy's Scouts. I joined the United State Air Force in 1965 and trained in Sebshin Kai Karate in India from 1966 to 1968, Registered at Selhin Kai Headquarter O Saha Japan and Headquarter H.M.A.F.

I Joined the Shotokan Warriors Assoc. in Bridgeport Conn. in 1969, and continued to Train in Free Style Karate. I received my 2nd Degree Black Belt in Shotokan Karate in 1975 from the Shotokan Warriors Assoc. of Bridgeport Conn., and started to teach Women Self-Defense Classes in the year 1971 when I received my 1st Degree Black Belt, at this time I opened two Karate Schools, Free Style and Shotokan Karate at the North End and Orcutt Boy's Club in Bridgeport Conn., and started an Institution for various Drug Free Programs. When I moved to St. Thomas V.I. in the year 1976 I opened my first Martial Arts Karate School and Drug Free Programs. at the Little School House. There after my first Promotion Ceremony, I started to Teach Martial Arts and Instituted Drug Free Programs at the various Community Centers.

DEVELOPMENT

I Started to Develop Jukan-Do Karate in Bridgeport Conn., in 1958 to the present Day. Jukan-Do Karate is for all Martial Artist, The way of ten. This form of Martial Arts consist of Basic, Self-Defense, Kata, Sparring, Bo Staff, Escrima Sticks, Samurai Sword, Sliding Block-Punching, Throwing Techniques, and Kick Boxing. Student must prepare one self for Jukan-Do Karate by Development of Exercise, Concentration, Focus, Speed, Strength, Timing, Balance, Flexibility, and Memory, Student must practice Daily and most strive for a common Goal, in time The body and mind will develop as one.

ACKNOWLEDGEMENT

I would like to give my profound gratitude to my Brother Master Charles Leonard for his dedication and continued support of my Martial Arts Schools on St. Thomas V.I., Master Charles Leonard trained over seas in Vietnam and Thailand in Martial Arts Karate and JuDo, and have Trained under me on St. Thomas in Shotokan and Free Style Karate for over 32 years.

MASTER CHARLES LEONARD

Beginning Class Session

1 . YOI DACHI READY STANCE

Stand with feet shoulder width apart, legs straight and toes facing forward, left arm center of body below abdomen, open left hand facing right, place front of right fist against open left hand, flat fist facing up.

2. BACK FIST OPEN PALM

Stand with feet shoulder width apart, legs straight, open left hand palm facing you, right back fist against open left palm, above head level.

3. DOUBLE OPEN PALM

Continue from step 2, turn both open hands above head level, facing outward, left open hand, on top of right open hand, fingers together to form a triangle.

LINES OF MOVEMENTS FOR KATAS

STRAIGHT LINE MOVEMENTS

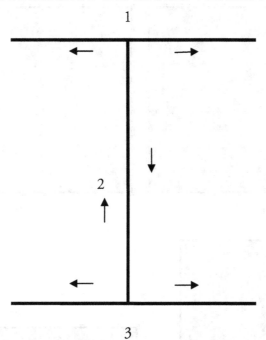

FIST AND HAND VIEWS

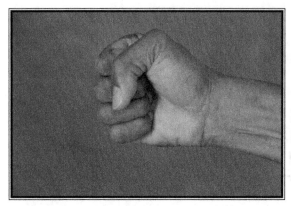

Close Fist

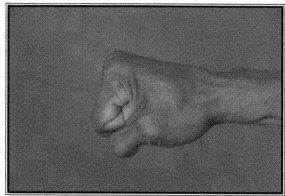

Top Fist

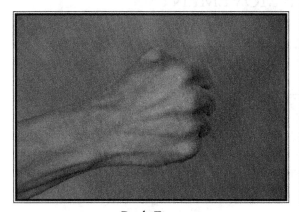

Back Fist

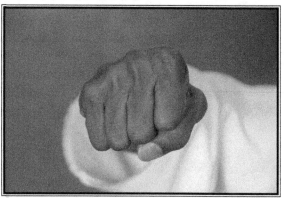

Front Fist

Bottom Fist

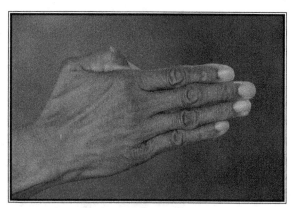

Flat Back Hand

PART I INTRODUCTION

Beginning Class Session

(Yoi Dachi) For Martial Arts

Students Only

YOI DACHI

4 5 6

FEET TOGETHER HANDS TO THE SIDE OF YOUR BODY.

4. and 5. From figure 3 move both hands in a circular motion to the side of your body, Bend both knees and Bow Slightly looking straight ahead. Figure 6, Standing in Yoi Dachi As illustrated in Figure 1.

2 BACK FIST OPEN PALM

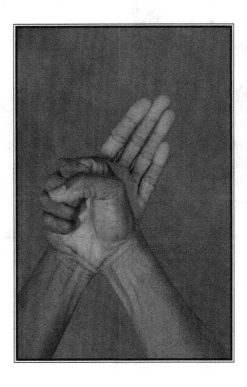

DOUBLE FIST CHAMBER

1. Place left close fist, facing down, on top of right close fist facing up, just above waist level, as illustrated in above picture.

OPEN HAND FIST CHAMBER

1 . Place right open hand on top of left close fist, facing up above waist level as illustrated in picture above.

PART 2 CALISTHENICS

Calisthenics

Jumping Jacks

Running In Place

SITTING JUMPING JACKS

1. Stand with feet together, hands to the side of body as shown in picture 1, jump up slightly and sit down in a position with legs apart, and hands above head, fingers touching each other, as shown in picture 2, go back to position 1 as shown in picture 3, repeat 10 times. Increase jumping jacks with muscle development.

CROSSLEG LEG JUMPING JACKS

1. Stand with feet shoulder width apart, hands to side of body, as shown in picture 1, jump up slightly off floor and place right foot in front of left foot 45 degrees angle to the right, knees bend, and hands above your head, fingers touching each other as shown in picture 2, jump back to position 1, as shown in picture 3, and repeat opposite leg as shown in picture 4. Five times each leg.

RUNNING IN PLACE

1. Standing with feet as wide as Shoulders, bring your right knee up to touch your right elbow, repeat opposite side, continue running in place, 10 times each leg, increase with body development.

PART 3 HAND & FIST PUSHUPS

Hand And Fist

Pushups

STRAIGHT FORWARD OPENHAND PUSHUPS

1. Place both feet and open hands approximately shoulder width apart, while In this straight forward pushup position, fingers open, facing forward, push your body up and come back down to original position, repeat 10 times and increase with arm and shoulder muscle development.

OUTSIDE OPENHAND PUSHUPS

1. Place both feet and open hands approximately shoulder width apart, while in this straight forward pushup position, fingers open, hands facing outward to the side of the body, push your body up and come back down to your original position, repeat 10 times and increase repetitions with arm and shoulder development.

1. Place both feet and hands approximately shoulder width apart, while in the straight forward pushup position, fingers together facing inward to each other, push your body straight up and come back down to original position, repeat 10 times and increase repetition with arm and muscle development.

FRONT FIST PUSHUPS

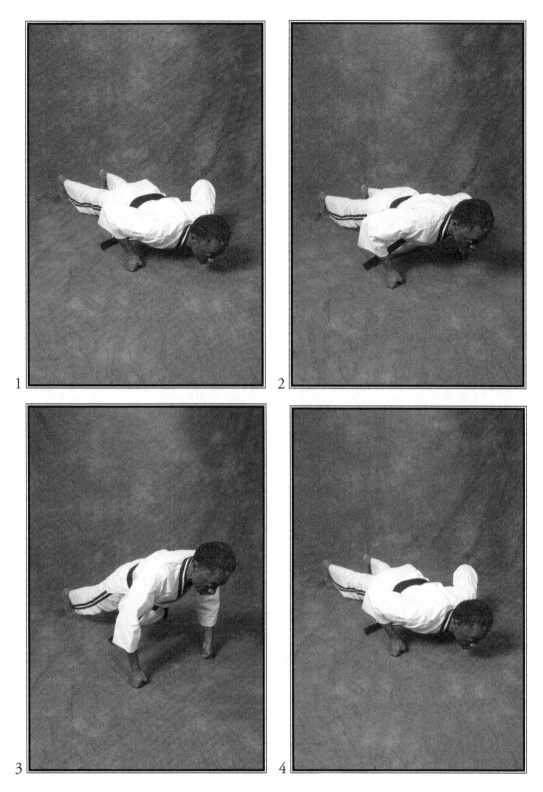

1. Place both feet and fist approximately shoulder width apart, while in a straight pushup position as shown in picture 1, with both fist in a vertical position on floor, push your body straight up as shown in picture 2 and 3, then come back down as shown in picture 4, repeat 10 times and increase pushups with arms and shoulder muscle development.

PART 4 HAND & FINGER EXERCISE

Hand And Finger

Exercise

VERTICAL ROTATING PALM
IN AND OUT FACING FRONT

1. Bring both arms up to shoulder level, palms facing out, fingers pointing in an upward Direction as in picture 1, rotate open hands clock wise and counter clock wise, five Rotations in each direction.

VERTICAL POSITION ROTATING FIST

1. Bring both arms up at shoulder level, proper fist facing each other, as in picture 1, rotate fist clock wise and counter clock wise as illustrated in picture 2 to 7, five rotations for each direction.

VERTICAL BACKFIST OPEN FINGERS

1. Standing with feet wide as shoulder, toes facing forward, hands straight in front, shoulder level, back fist to back fist, picture 1, open fingers and close, picture 2. and3. Repeat 10 times.

Vertical Facing Oprn Fingers Exercise

1

2

3

1.Standing with feet wide as shoulders, toes facing forward, arms straight in front of body, shoulder level, flat fist facing each other picture 1, open fingers and close, picture 2 and 3, repeat 10 times.

PART 5 WINDMILL EXERCISE

Windmill Exercise

STANDING WINDMILL

1. While standing with both legs straight, wider than shoulder's and both arms out straight at shoulder level at left and right side of body, palms facing down, as in picture 1, bend over and touch your lrft foot with your right hand picture 2, and back to position as in picture 1 , go to picture 3, picture 4 is the opposite of picture 2, go to picture 5, repeat 10 times.

Standing Windmill Rotation Left To Right

1. Standing with feet wider than shoulder, and arms straight out to your side, Palms facing down, as in picture 1, turn to your left and then turn to your right As in picture 2 and 3, and then back to position 4, repeat 10 times.

Standing Windmill Elbow To Knee

1. Standing with feet wider than shoulder, both hands together behind your head, picture1, bend over and touch your left knee with right elbow, as in picture 2, and back up to picture 3 position, now bend over and touch your left elbow to your right knee and back up as in picture 5, repeat 10 times.

PART 6 LEG LIFTS

Leg Lifts

1. Stand with feet shoulder width apart, left side fist chamber, right arm straight out at shoulder level, open hand, palm facing down, bring right foot up and touch open right hand, picture 1 and 2, repeat same on left side of body, picture 3 and 4, leg lift ten times each side.

1. Place your left foot approximately three steps in front of right foot, shoulder width, left fist in a left side chamber, right open hand, palm facing down, arm at shoulder level in front of you, picture 1, now bring your right foot straight up and touch the fingers of your right hand as shown in picture 2, and then back to position shown in picture 1, repeat 10 times, picture 3 and 4, opposite side.

PART 7 HOP, JUMP, AND CRAWL

Bunny Hop

Kangaroo Jump

Aligator Crawl

1. Sit down as close as possible to the floor with both hands behind your back as shown in picture 1 . then jump up as high as possible with knees up to waist level as shown in picture 2, and back down as shown in picture 3, repeat 5 times moving forward.

1. While in a sitting position, feet as wide as shoulder's, both hands behind your back one on top of the other, as shown in picture 1 , jump up forward with your legs and knees as illustrated in picture 2, and back to position 1 as shown in picture 3.

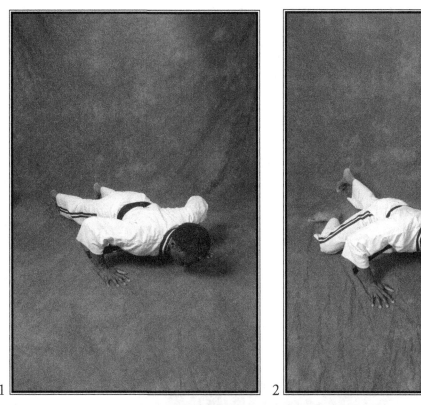

1. While in a push up position, flat open hands, fingers facing, forward, as in picture 1, start to move your body forward, side to side, as in picture 2 and 3, pushing with the knee that in bended, 6 movements forward.

PART 8 FLAT BACK SITUPS

Flatback Situps

Flatback Fingure To Toe Situps

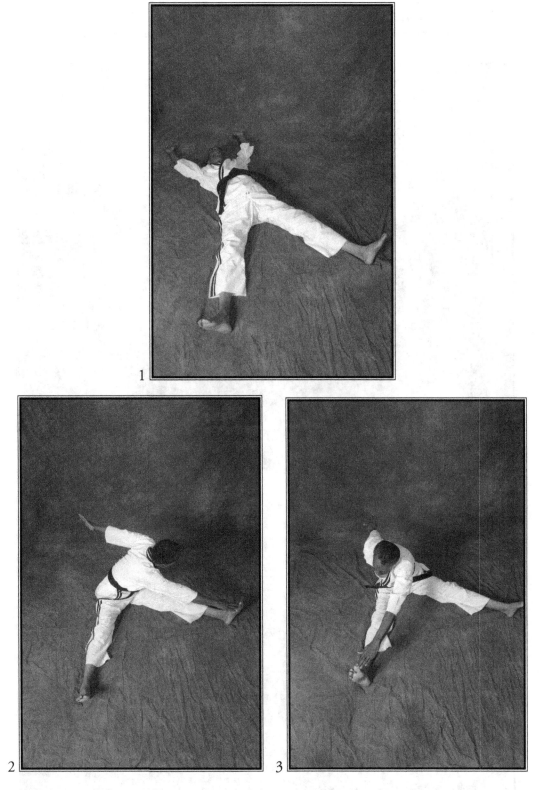

1. While flat on your back, open hands above your head, feet wider than shoulders as shown in picture 1, bring your body straight up in a sitting position and touch your left toes with open right hand picture 2, and then touch your right toes with open left hand picture 3, and then back to position in picture 1, repeat 10 times increase with muscle development.

FLATBACK ELBOW TO KNEE

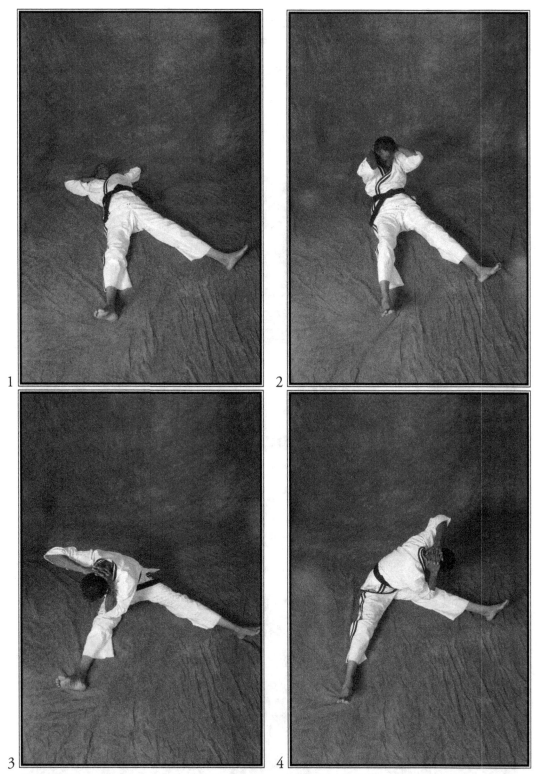

1. While flat on your back, hands behind your head and feet wide as Possible, as shown in picture 1, Bring your body up in a sitting position figure 2, hands still behind your head, turn body to right and bend over and touch your right knee, with left elbow, as in figure3, then go back to illustration1, then repeat 2 and touch right elbow to left knee, as shown in figure4. Repeat 10 times and increase with advance training.

FLATBACK BENDKNEE SITUPS

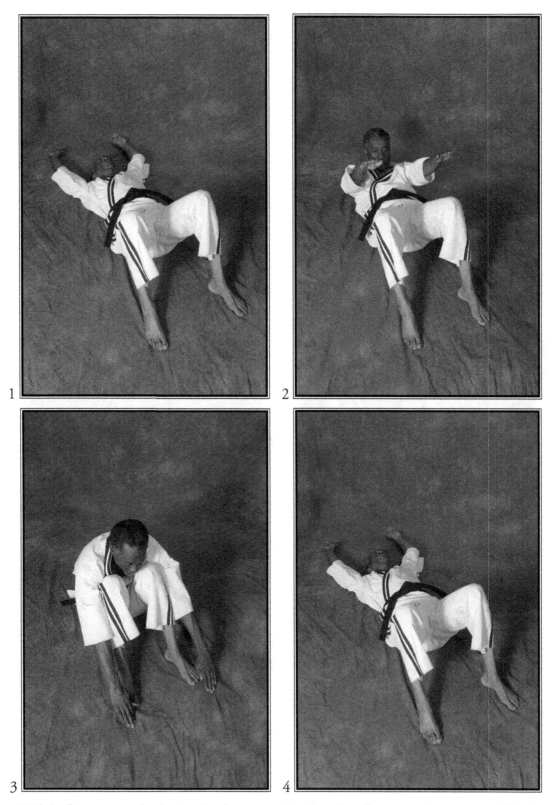

1.While flat on your back, hands above your head, palms facing up, knees in an (A), shape position as in illustration 1, bring both hands straight up above your head, and touch in front of your toes, as in figure3, and then go back to position1, repeat 10 times and advance with abdominal development.

PART 9 FLOOR LEG STRETCH

Flatback Leg Stretch

Flatback Frontleg Strectch

1. Have Student lay flat on back with hands extended v Shape away from head, lift left leg straight up and have individual hold ankle area with both hands and push left leg toward your body as far as possible until acknowledgement, as shown in picture 1, repeat with right foot as shown in picture 2.

SIDEBODY SIDELEG STRETCH

1.Have Student lay on right side, right hand extended out straight, place left hand on upper right arm area, and have individual lift left leg straight up until acknowledgement, repeat same opposite side.

FACEDOWN BACKLEG STRETCH

1. Have Student lay flat on belly, hands extended straight out in front, raising left leg up, knee slightly bend, individual with knees slightly bended places left hand under student left knee, and hold lower left leg with right hand and pull left knee up with left hand, as far up as possible until acknowledgement from student, as shown in picture 1, repeat opposite side as shown in picture 2.